J.S.Bach

for FINGERSTYLE UKULELE

Arrangements by John Nicholson

ISBN 978-1-4584-4603-9

7777 W. BLUEMOUND RD. P.O. BOX 13819 MILWAUKEE, WI 53213

In Australia Contact:
Hal Leonard Australia Pty. Ltd.
4 Lentara Court
Cheltenham, Victoria, 3192 Australia
Email: ausadmin@halleonard.com.au

Visit Hal Leonard Online at
www.halleonard.com

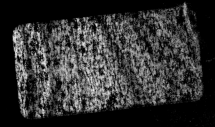

CONTENTS

Be Thou with Me

By Johann Sebastian Bach

*Low G tuning:
(low to high) G-C-E-A

Moderately slow

*G string tuned down one octave.

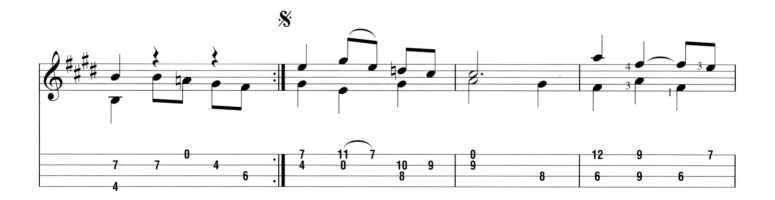

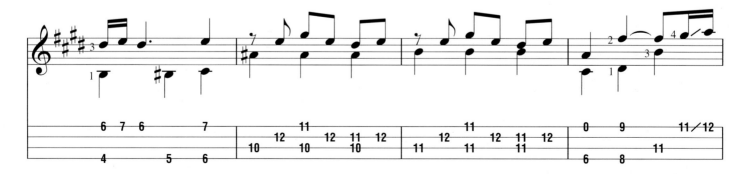

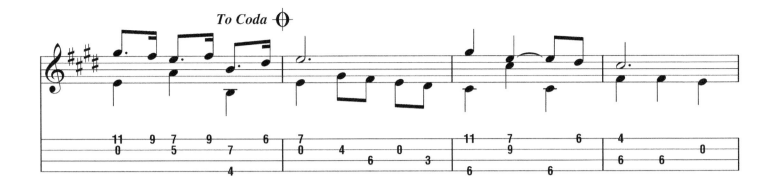

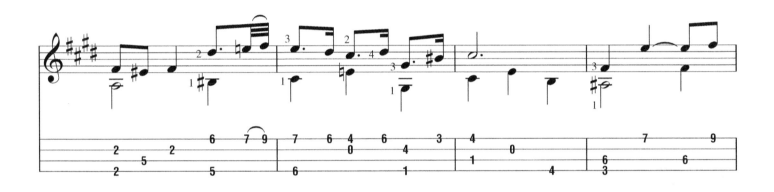

Bourrée

from SUITE NO. 1 IN E MINOR FOR LUTE

By Johann Sebastian Bach

Moderately

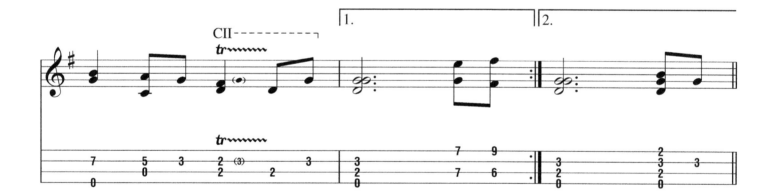

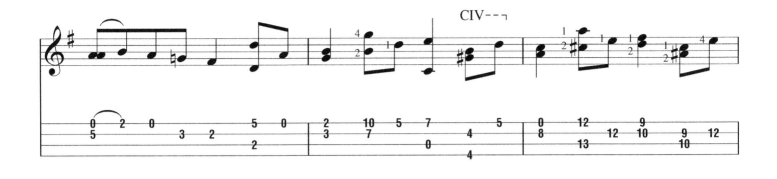

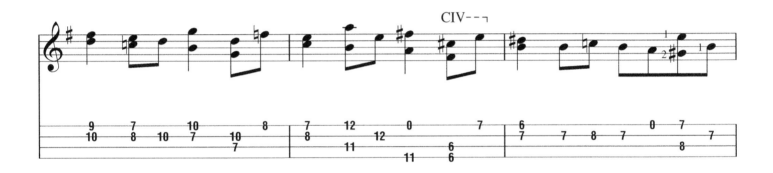

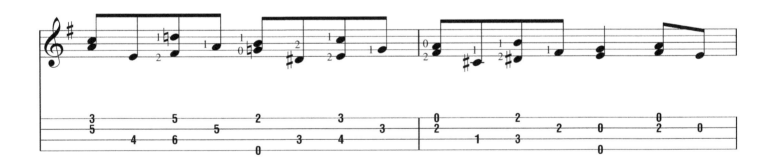

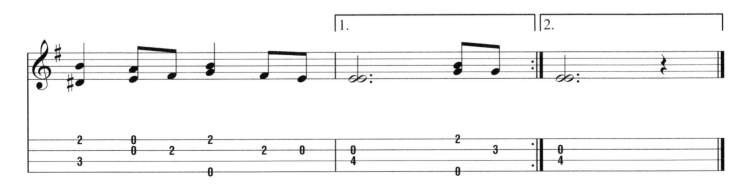

Arioso

By Johann Sebastian Bach

*Low G tuning:
(low to high) G-C-E-A

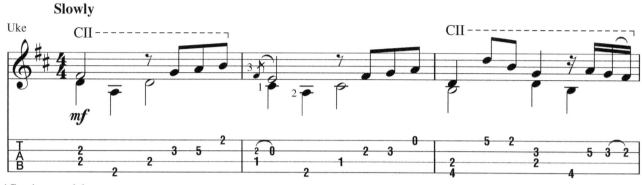

*G string tuned down one octave.

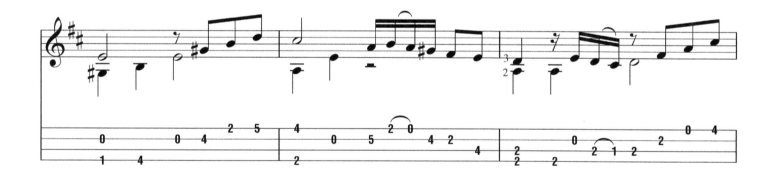

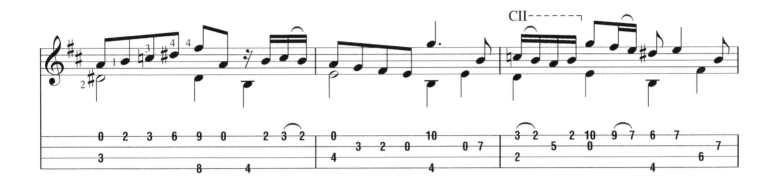

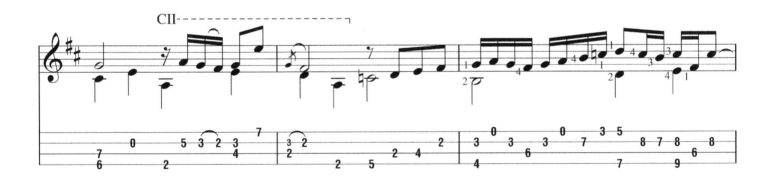

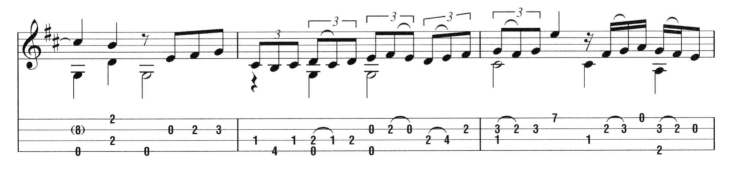

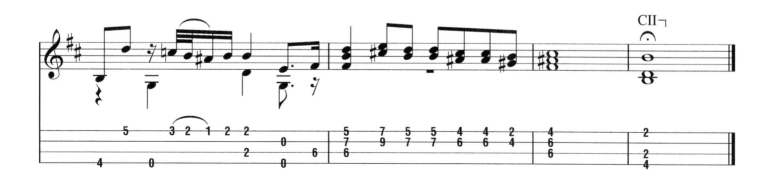

10

Chorale in C Major, BWV 514

By Johann Sebastian Bach

Moderately

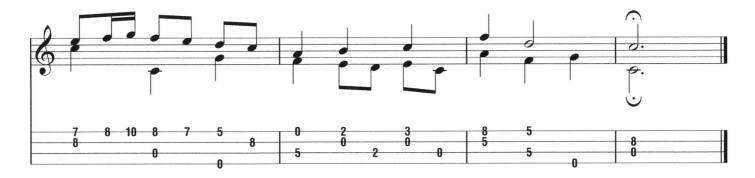

Little Prelude No. 2 in C Major

By Johann Sebastian Bach

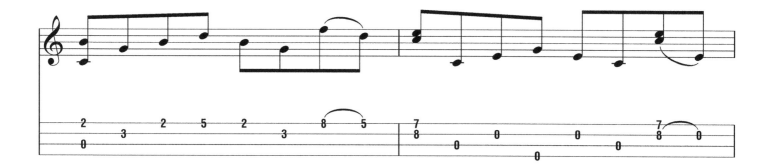

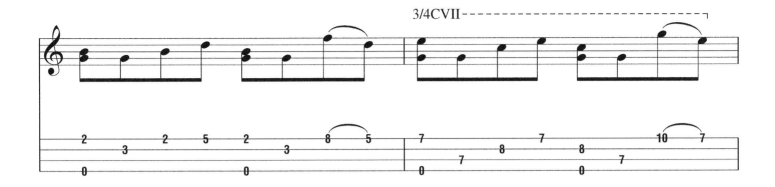

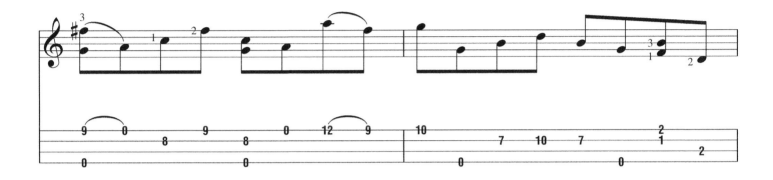

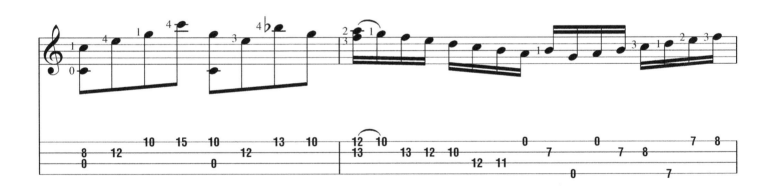

Minuet in G

from the ANNA MAGDALENA NOTEBOOK

By Johann Sebastian Bach

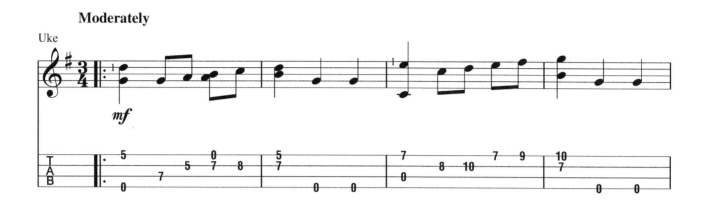

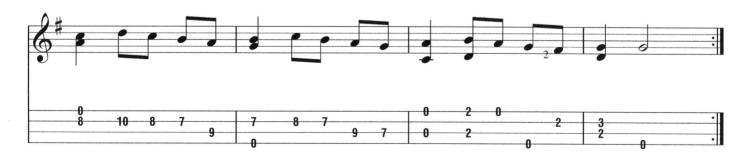

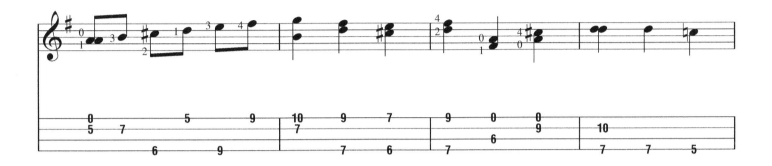

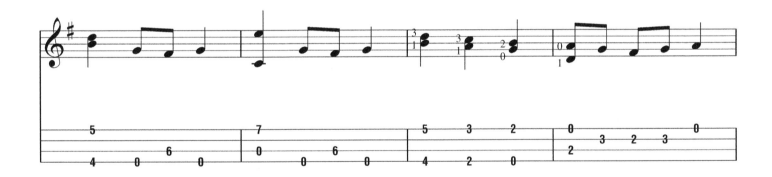

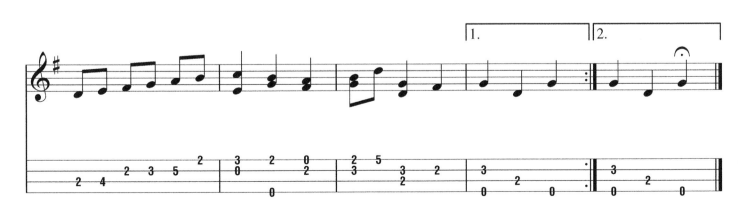

15

Minuet I, BWV 813

from FRENCH SUITE NO. 2 IN C MINOR

By Johann Sebastian Bach

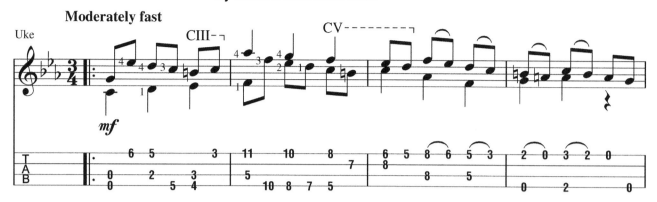

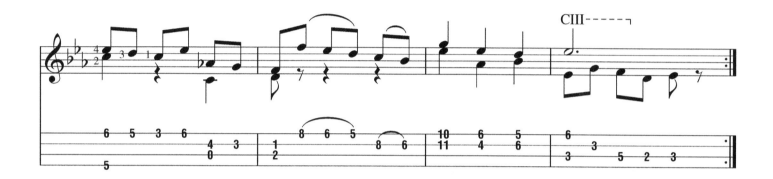

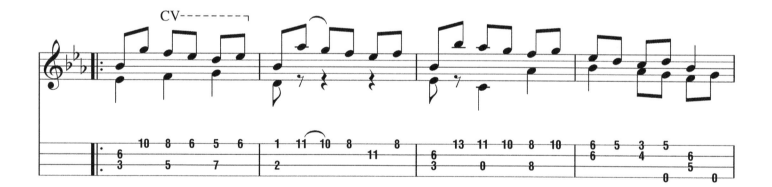

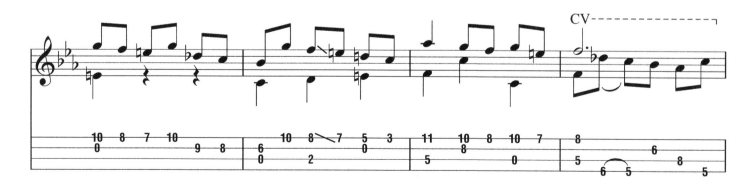

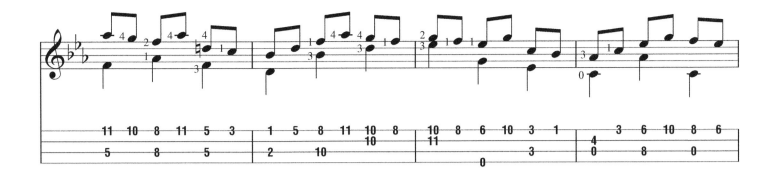

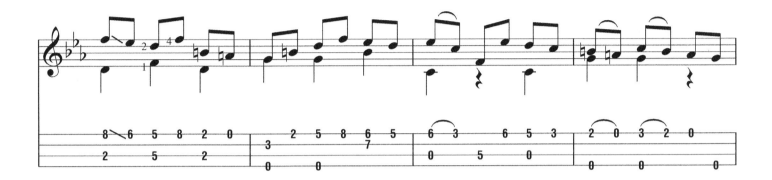

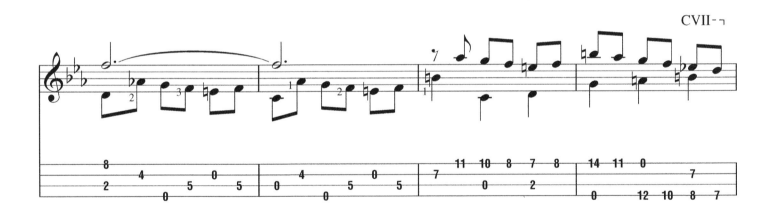

CVII-⌐

Musette in D Major

from the LITTLE CLAVIER BOOK FOR ANNA MAGDALENA BACH
By Johann Sebastian Bach

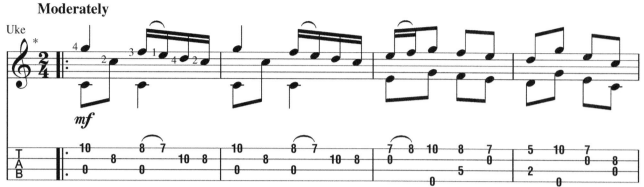

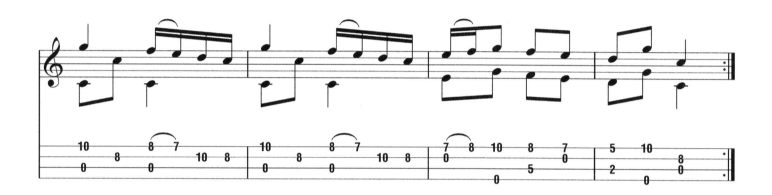

*This arrangement in C major for playability.

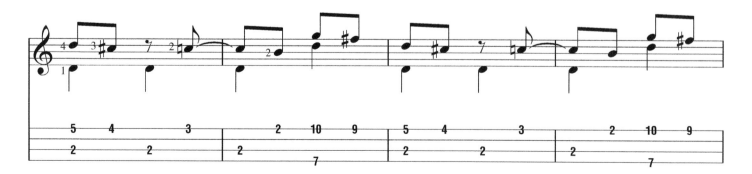

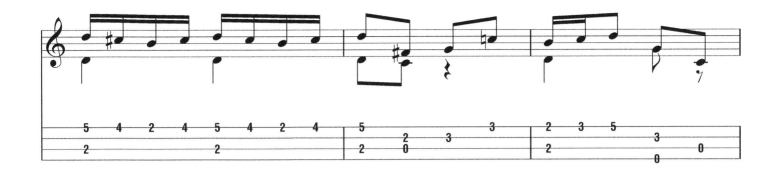

Jesu, Joy of Man's Desiring

By Johann Sebastian Bach

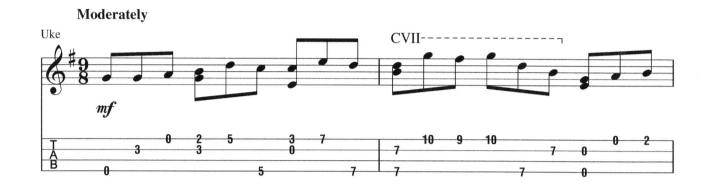

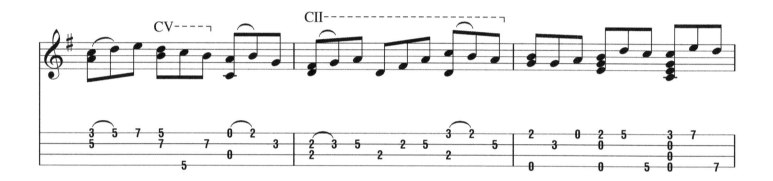

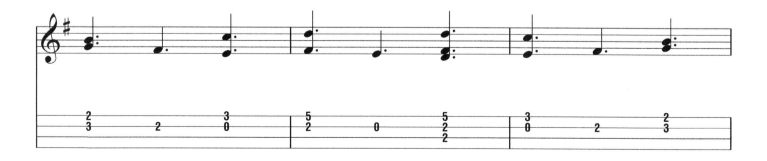

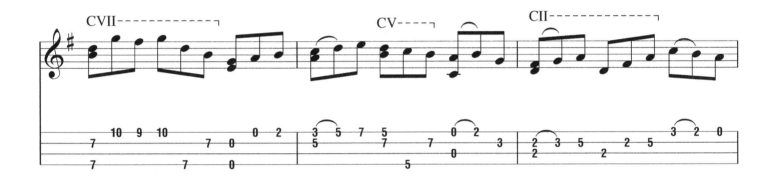

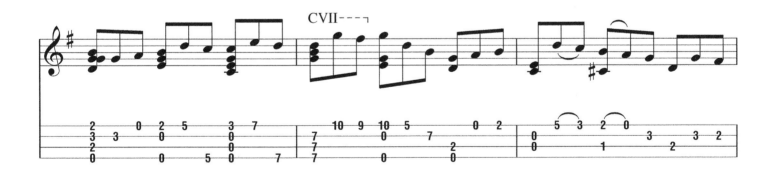

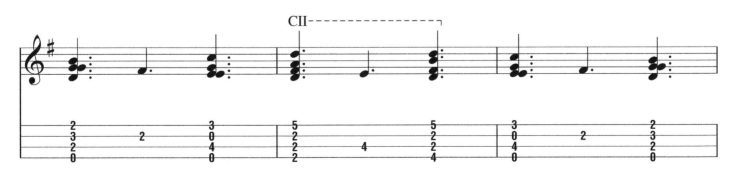

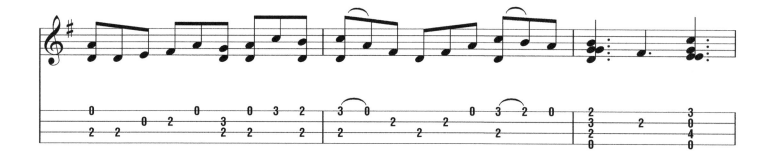

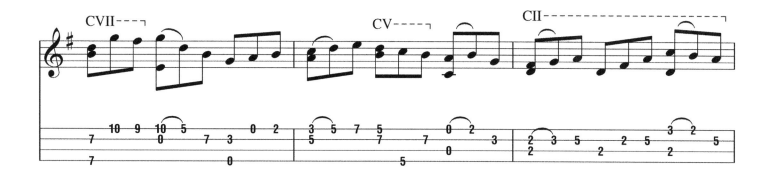

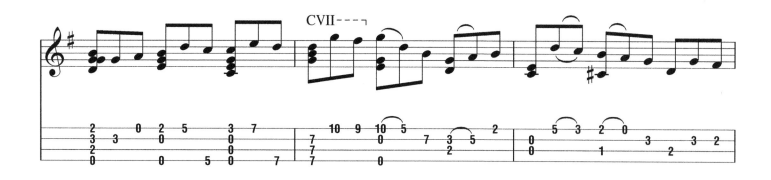

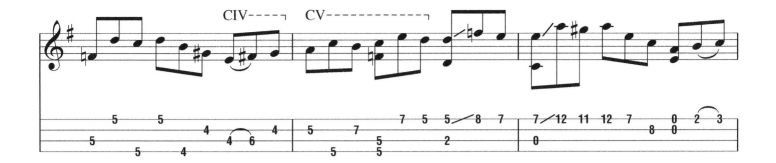

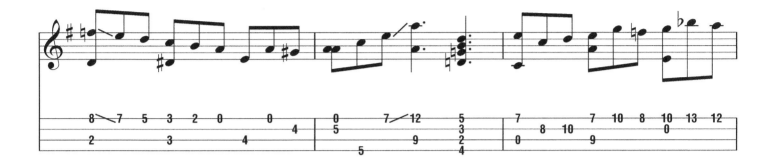

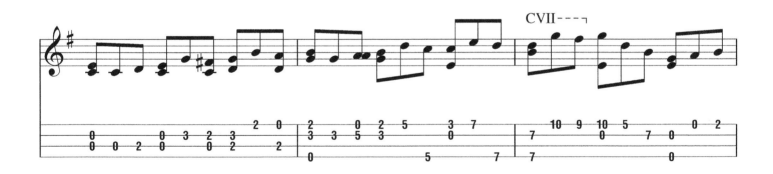

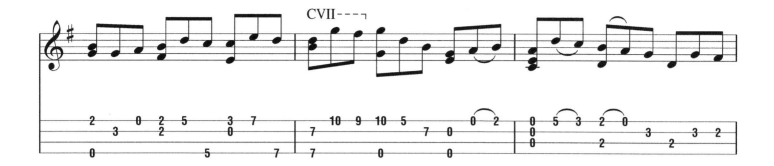

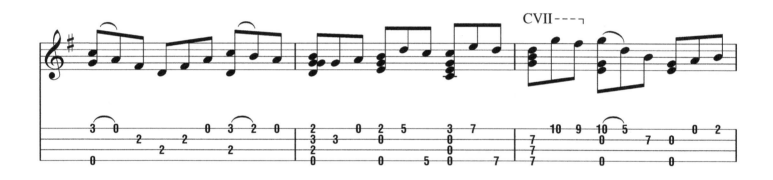

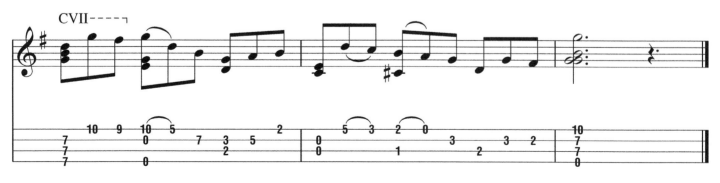

Prelude
(Cello Suite No. 1)
By Johann Sebastian Bach

Moderately slow

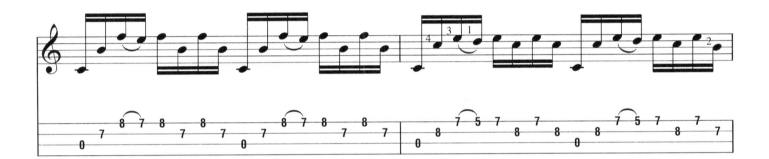

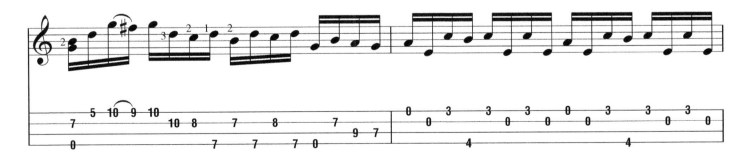

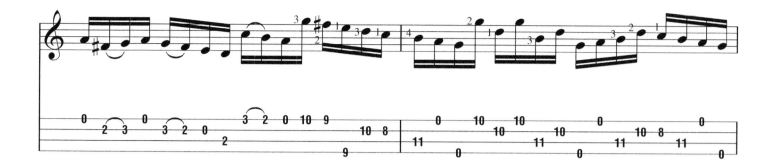

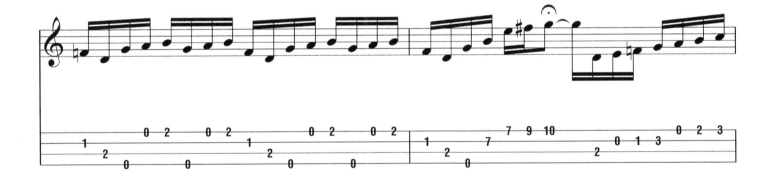

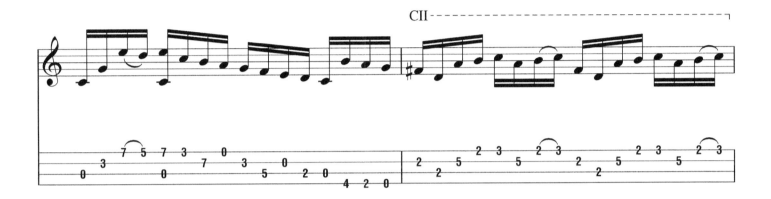

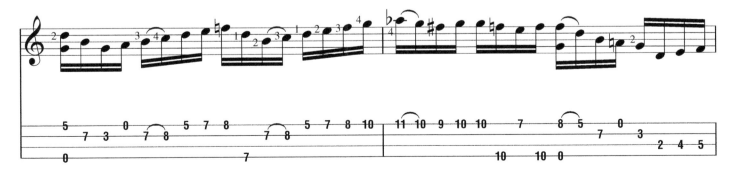

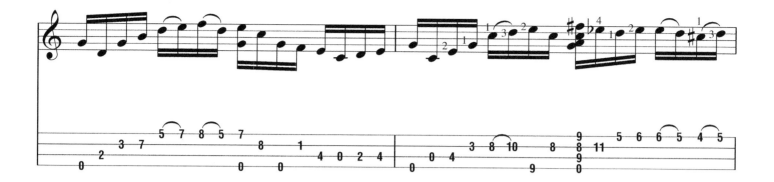

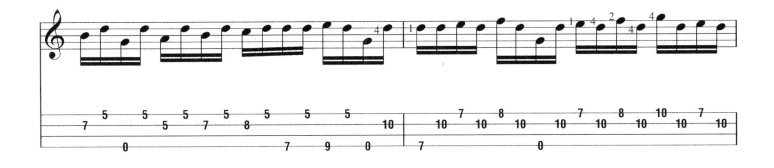

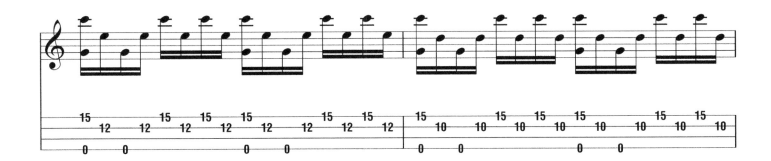

Prelude in C Major

from THE WELL-TEMPERED CLAVIER, BOOK 1
By Johann Sebastian Bach

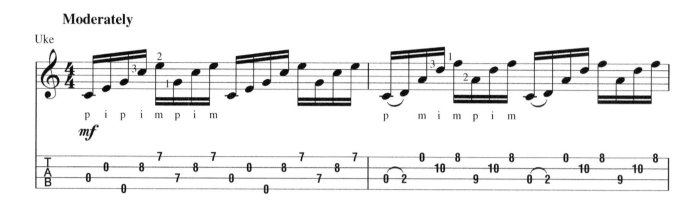

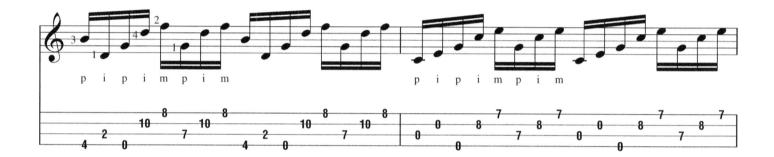

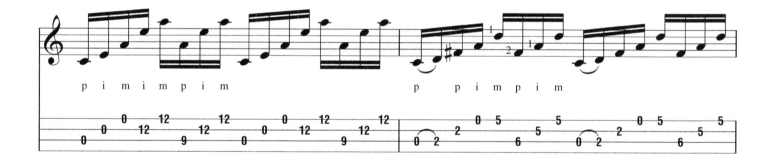

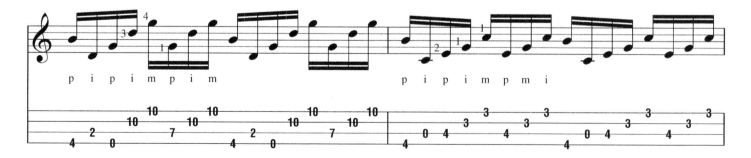

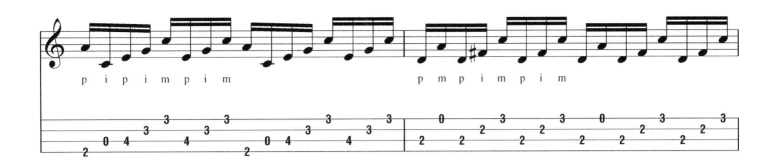

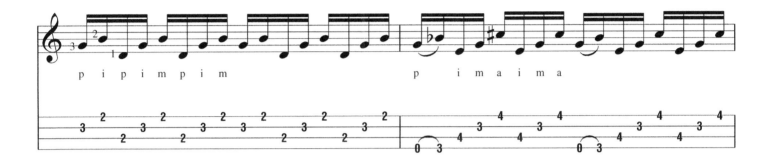

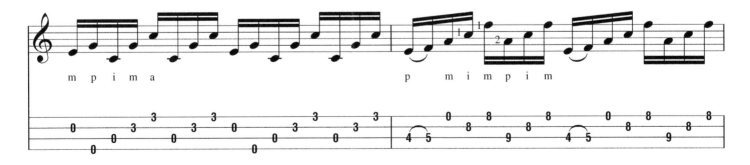

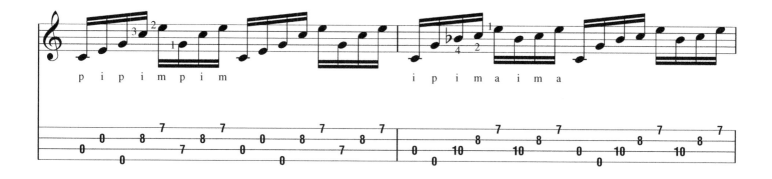

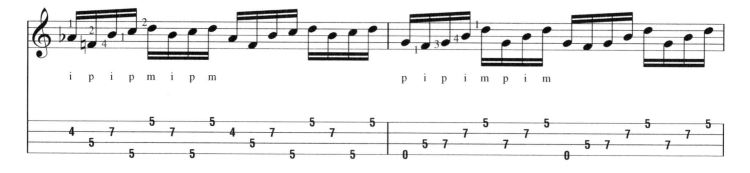

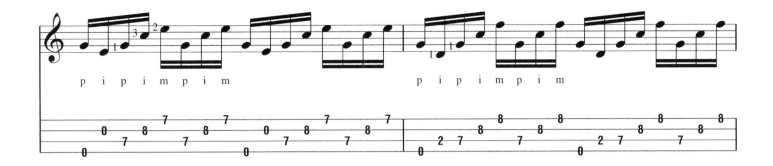

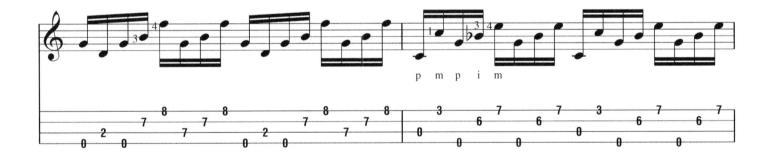

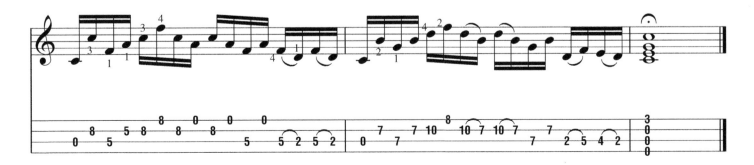

Quia Respexit

from MAGNIFICAT

By Johann Sebastian Bach

Moderately, in 2

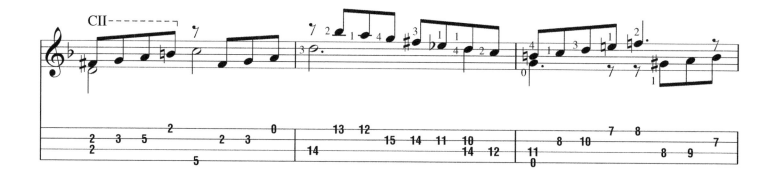

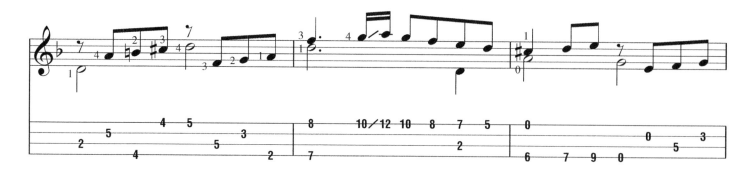

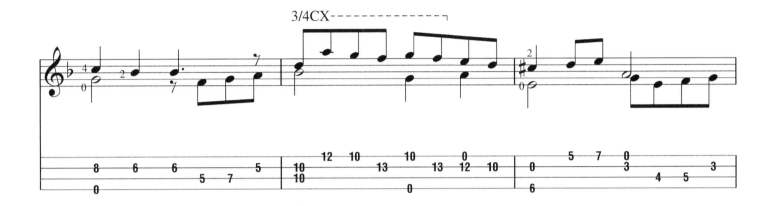

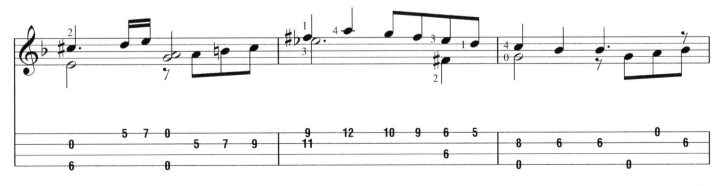

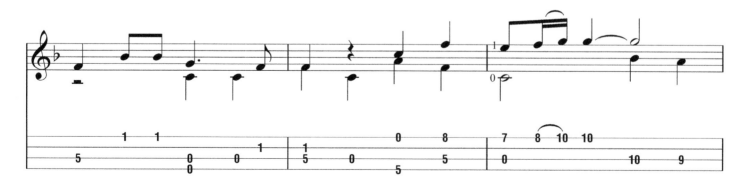

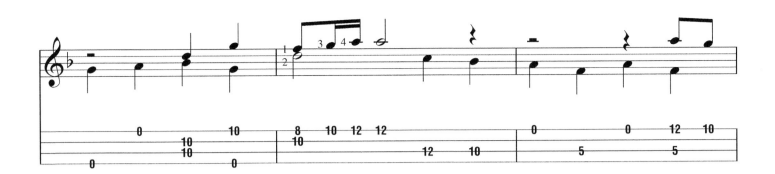

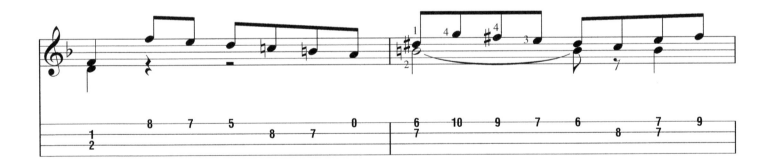

Sleepers, Awake
(Wachet Auf)

from CANTATA NO. 140
By Johann Sebastian Bach

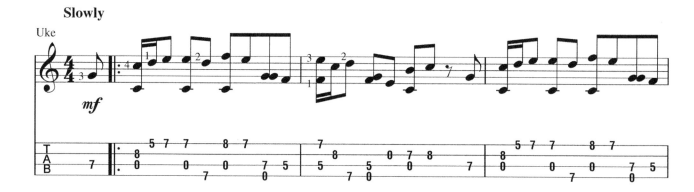

38

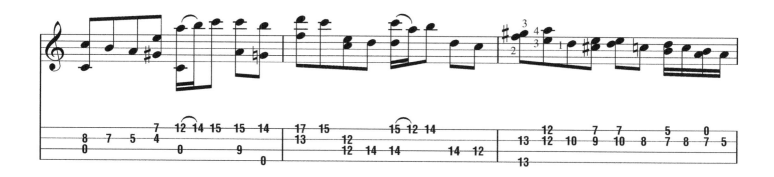

40

Violin Partita No. 1, BWV 1002
"Tempo di Bourrée"

By Johann Sebastian Bach

*Low G tuning:
(low to high) G-C-E-A

Moderately fast

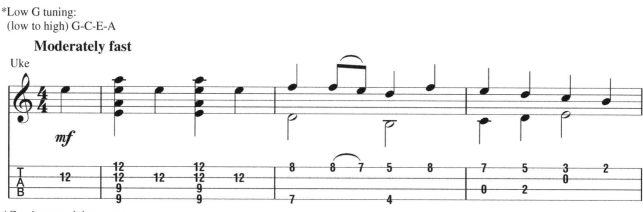

*G string tuned down one octave.

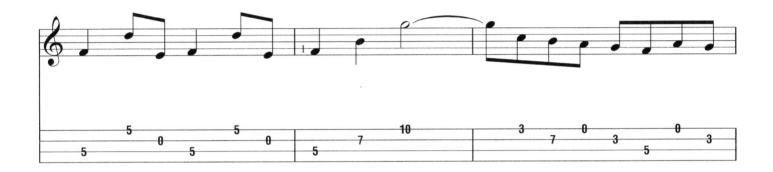

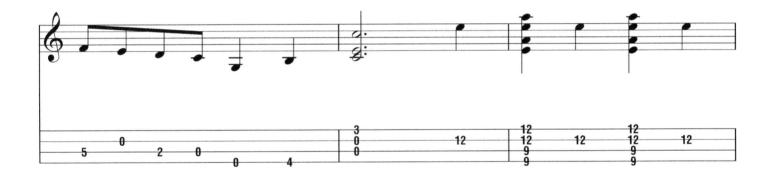

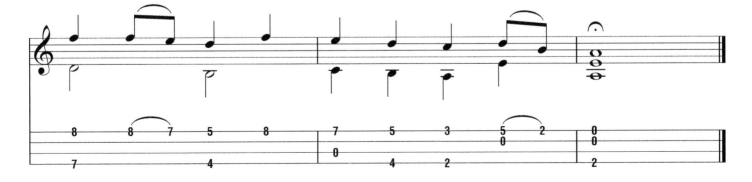

Sheep May Safely Graze

from CANTATA NO. 208
By Johann Sebastian Bach

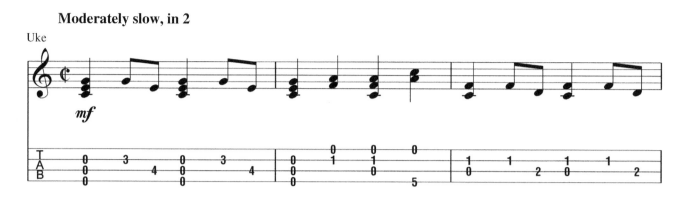

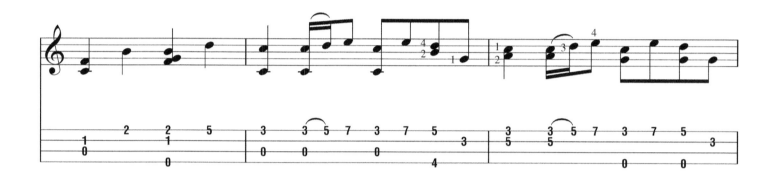

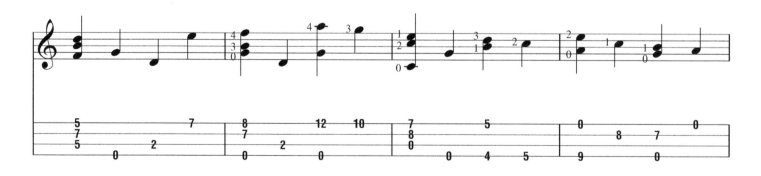

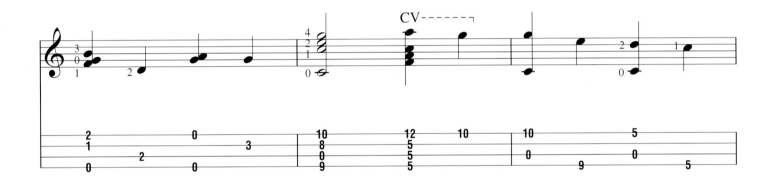

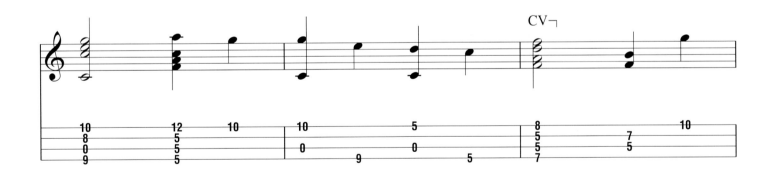

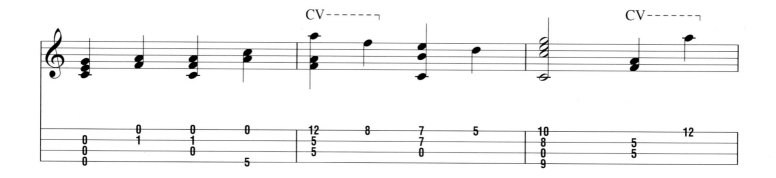

The Best Collections for Ukulele

The Best Songs Ever

70 songs have now been arranged for ukulele. Includes: Always • Bohemian Rhapsody • Memory • My Favorite Things • Over the Rainbow • Piano Man • What a Wonderful World • Yesterday • You Raise Me Up • and more.

00282413........$17.99

Campfire Songs for Ukulele

30 favorites to sing as you roast marshmallows and strum your uke around the campfire. Includes: God Bless the U.S.A. • Hallelujah • The House of the Rising Sun • I Walk the Line • Puff the Magic Dragon • Wagon Wheel • You Are My Sunshine • and more.

00129170 ......$14.99

The Daily Ukulele

arr. Liz and Jim Beloff
Strum a different song everyday with easy arrangements of 365 of your favorite songs in one big songbook! Includes favorites by the Beatles, Beach Boys, and Bob Dylan, folk songs, pop songs, kids' songs, Christmas carols, and Broadway and Hollywood tunes, all with a spiral binding for ease of use.

00240356 Original Edition.................$39.99
00240681 Leap Year Edition $39.99
00119270 Portable Edition $37.50

Disney Hits for Ukulele

Play 23 of your favorite Disney songs on your ukulele. Includes: The Bare Necessities • Cruella De Vil • Do You Want to Build a Snowman? • Kiss the Girl • Lava • Let It Go • Once upon a Dream • A Whole New World • and more.

00151250 ......$16.99

Also available:
00291547 **Disney Fun Songs for Ukulele** ...$16.99
00701708 **Disney Songs for Ukulele**.......$14.99
00334696 **First 50 Disney Songs on Ukulele** .$16.99

First 50 Songs You Should Play on Ukulele

An amazing collec-tion of 50 accessible, must-know favorites: Edelweiss • Hey, Soul Sister • I Walk the Line • I'm Yours • Imagine • Over the Rainbow • Peaceful Easy Feeling • The Rainbow Connection • Riptide • more.

00149250 ....$16.99
Also available:
00292082 **First 50 Melodies on Ukulele** ...$15.99
00289029 **First 50 Songs on Solo Ukulele**..$15.99
00347437 **First 50 Songs to Strum on Uke** .$16.99

40 Most Streamed Songs for Ukulele

40 top hits that sound great on uke! Includes: Despacito • Feel It Still • Girls like You • Happier • Havana • High Hopes • The Middle • Perfect • 7 Rings • Shallow • Shape of You • Something Just like This • Stay • Sucker • Sunflower • Sweet but Psycho • Thank U, Next • There's Nothing Holdin' Me Back • Without Me • and more!

00298113 ....$17.99

The 4 Chord Songbook

With just 4 chords, you can play 50 hot songs on your ukulele! Songs include: Brown Eyed Girl • Do Wah Diddy Diddy • Hey Ya! • Ho Hey • Jessie's Girl • Let It Be • One Love • Stand by Me • Toes • With or Without You • and many more.

00142050........$16.99

Also available:
00141143 **The 3-Chord Songbook**........$16.99

Pop Songs for Kids

30 easy pop favorites for kids to play on uke, including: Brave • Can't Stop the Feeling! • Feel It Still • Fight Song • Happy • Havana • House of Gold • How Far I'll Go • Let It Go • Remember Me (Ernesto de la Cruz) • Rewrite the Stars • Roar • Shake It Off • Story of My Life • What Makes You Beautiful • and more.

00284415...........................$16.99

Simple Songs for Ukulele

50 favorites for standard G-C-E-A ukulele tuning, including: All Along the Watchtower • Can't Help Falling in Love • Don't Worry, Be Happy • Ho Hey • I'm Yours • King of the Road • Sweet Home Alabama • You Are My Sunshine • and more.

00156815........$14.99
Also available:
00276644 **More Simple Songs for Ukulele** .$14.99

Top Hits of 2020

18 uke-friendly tunes of 2020 are featured in this collection of melody, lyric and chord arrangements in standard G-C-E-A tuning. Includes: Adore You (Harry Styles) • Before You Go (Lewis Capaldi) • Cardigan (Taylor Swift) • Daisies (Katy Perry) • I Dare You (Kelly Clarkson) • Level of Concern (twenty one pilots) • No Time to Die (Billie Eilish) • Rain on Me (Lady Gaga feat. Ariana Grande) • Say So (Doja Cat) • and more.

00355553...........................$14.99
Also available:
00302274 **Top Hits of 2019** $14.99

Ukulele: The Most Requested Songs

Strum & Sing Series
Cherry Lane Music
Nearly 50 favorites all expertly arranged for ukulele! Includes: Bubbly • Build Me Up, Buttercup • Cecilia • Georgia on My Mind • Kokomo • L-O-V-E • Your Body Is a Wonderland • and more.

02501453...........................$14.99

The Ultimate Ukulele Fake Book

Uke enthusiasts will love this giant, spiral-bound collection of over 400 songs for uke! Includes: Crazy • Dancing Queen • Downtown • Fields of Gold • Happy • Hey Jude • 7 Years • Summertime • Thinking Out Loud • Thriller • Wagon Wheel • and more.

00175500 9" x 12" Edition $45.00
00319997 5.5" x 8.5" Edition $39.99

Order today from your favorite music retailer at
halleonard.com

Prices, contents and availability subject to change without notice

Disney characters and artwork TM & © 2021 Disney

0621
479

HAL•LEONARD®
UKULELE PLAY-ALONG

Now you can play your favorite songs on your uke with great-sounding backing tracks to help you sound like a bona fide pro! The audio also features playback tools so you can adjust the tempo without changing the pitch and loop challenging parts.

1. POP HITS
00701451 Book/CD Pack $15.99

3. HAWAIIAN FAVORITES
00701453 Book/Online Audio $14.99

4. CHILDREN'S SONGS
00701454 Book/Online Audio $14.99

5. CHRISTMAS SONGS
00701696 Book/CD Pack $12.99

6. LENNON & MCCARTNEY
00701723 Book/Online Audio $12.99

7. DISNEY FAVORITES
00701724 Book/Online Audio $14.99

8. CHART HITS
00701745 Book/CD Pack $15.99

9. THE SOUND OF MUSIC
00701784 Book/CD Pack $14.99

10. MOTOWN
00701964 Book/CD Pack $12.99

11. CHRISTMAS STRUMMING
00702458 Book/Online Audio $12.99

12. BLUEGRASS FAVORITES
00702584 Book/CD Pack $12.99

13. UKULELE SONGS
00702599 Book/CD Pack $12.99

14. JOHNNY CASH
00702615 Book/Online Audio $15.99

15. COUNTRY CLASSICS
00702834 Book/CD Pack $12.99

16. STANDARDS
00702835 Book/CD Pack $12.99

17. POP STANDARDS
00702836 Book/CD Pack $12.99

18. IRISH SONGS
00703086 Book/Online Audio $12.99

19. BLUES STANDARDS
00703087 Book/CD Pack $12.99

20. FOLK POP ROCK
00703088 Book/CD Pack $12.99

21. HAWAIIAN CLASSICS
00703097 Book/CD Pack $12.99

22. ISLAND SONGS
00703098 Book/CD Pack $12.99

23. TAYLOR SWIFT
00221966 Book/Online Audio $16.99

24. WINTER WONDERLAND
00101871 Book/CD Pack $12.99

25. GREEN DAY
00110398 Book/CD Pack $14.99

26. BOB MARLEY
00110399 Book/Online Audio $14.99

27. TIN PAN ALLEY
00116358 Book/CD Pack $12.99

28. STEVIE WONDER
00116736 Book/CD Pack $14.99

29. OVER THE RAINBOW & OTHER FAVORITES
00117076 Book/Online Audio $15.99

30. ACOUSTIC SONGS
00122336 Book/CD Pack $14.99

31. JASON MRAZ
00124166 Book/CD Pack $14.99

32. TOP DOWNLOADS
00127507 Book/CD Pack $14.99

33. CLASSICAL THEMES
00127892 Book/Online Audio $14.99

34. CHRISTMAS HITS
00128602 Book/CD Pack $14.99

35. SONGS FOR BEGINNERS
00129009 Book/Online Audio $14.99

36. ELVIS PRESLEY HAWAII
00138199 Book/Online Audio $14.99

37. LATIN
00141191 Book/Online Audio $14.99

38. JAZZ
00141192 Book/Online Audio $14.99

39. GYPSY JAZZ
00146559 Book/Online Audio $15.99

40. TODAY'S HITS
00160845 Book/Online Audio $14.99

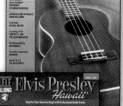

HAL•LEONARD®
www.halleonard.com

Prices, contents, and availability subject to change without notice.